RAND M?NALLY

Primary **Atlas**
4ᵗʰ Edition

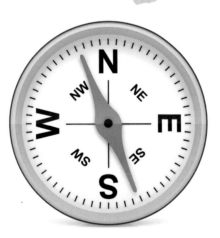

Digital Resources Available

This Atlas includes access to a library of digital resources including outline maps, worksheets, guides and much more. Simply enter the link below in a browser to access all the resources.

http://www.randmcnally.com/EDU00469

ISBN: 0-528-00469-7

Maps

An **atlas** is a book of **maps**.

Maps use colors, lines, and shapes to show real places on Earth.

The lines, colors, and shapes are called **symbols**.

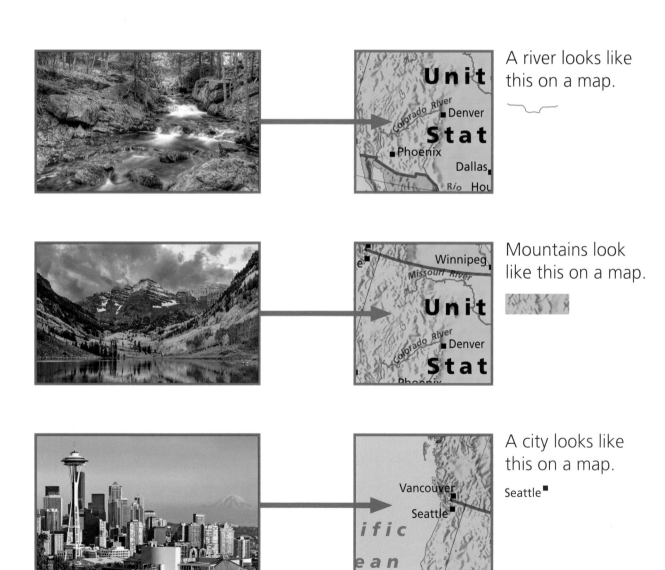

A river looks like this on a map.

Mountains look like this on a map.

A city looks like this on a map.

Seattle ■

A map legend tells us about symbols.

What symbols do you see in this legend?

North America

——————	Country boundary
∿	River
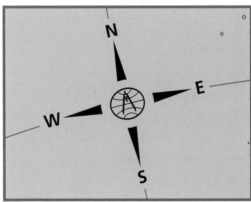	Mountains
United States	Country
✪ Washington, D.C.	Country capital
▪ Seattle	City
Atlantic Ocean	Ocean

You can find directions on a map. The **compass rose** shows North, East, South, and West.

The United States

The United States is our country.
Can you find your state?

Map Skills

Name a place south of your state.

▲ This is the Golden Gate Bridge in San Francisco.

▲ This is Mt. Rushmore in South Dakota.

▲ This is the White House in Washington, D.C.

United States

▬▬▬	Country boundary
———	State boundary
～～	River
[mountains]	Mountains
Canada	Country
New Mexico	State
✪ Washington, D.C.	Country capital
★ Lincoln	State capital

The World

Our world has many countries.
Most countries are on large land areas
called continents.

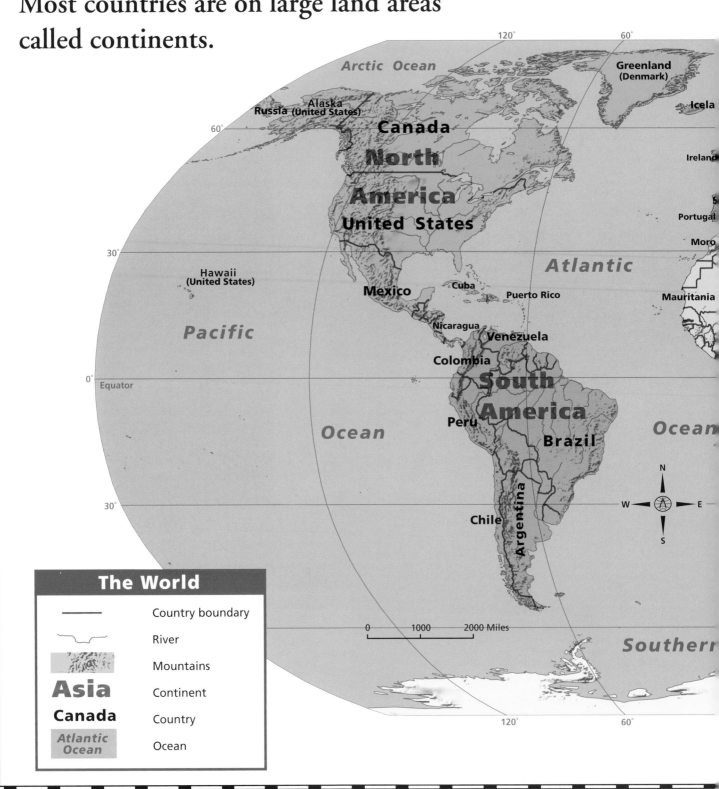

	The World
——	Country boundary
⌄	River
	Mountains
Asia	Continent
Canada	Country
Atlantic Ocean	Ocean

Map Skills

What continent is north of South America?

Arctic Ocean

Russia

Europe

Asia

Kazakhstan

Mongolia

Poland

Ukraine

Italy

Greece Turkey

Iran

China

South Korea

Japan

Iraq

Pakistan

Libya

Egypt

Saudi Arabia

India

Taiwan

Pacific

Africa

Oman

Chad Sudan

Yemen

Thailand

Philippines

Ocean

South Sudan Ethiopia

Malaysia

Equator

Kenya

Dem. Rep. of the Congo

Tanzania

Indonesia

Papua New Guinea

Angola

Zambia

Indian

Zimbabwe Madagascar

Namibia

Botswana

Australia

South Africa

Ocean

Australia

New Zealand

Ocean

Antarctica

© Rand McNally
Made in U.S.A.
M-101055-4

North America

North America is the continent where we live.

This lighthouse is in Canada.

This Aztec pyramid is in Mexico.

North America

————	Country boundary
	River
	Mountains
United States	Country
✴ Washington, D.C.	Country capital
■ Seattle	City
Atlantic Ocean	Ocean

South America

Most of South America is south of the Equator.

This river runs through a rainforest in Brazil.

This girl and llama live in Peru.

South America

———	Country boundary
∿	River
▨	Mountains
Brazil	Country
⊛ Lima	Country capital
■ Sao Paulo	City
Atlantic Ocean	Ocean

Europe

Europe is a small continent with many countries.

The Parthenon is a famous building in Greece.

This is St. Basil's Cathedral in Russia.

This is the Eiffel Tower in France.

This castle is in Germany.

Reykjavik **Iceland**

Atlantic

Ocean

SCOTLAND

NORTHERN IRELAND

Ireland
Dublin

WALES ENGLAND

United Kingd

London

Amste

English Channel Bel

Luxemb
Seine Par

Loire River

France

Portugal **Spain**
Lisbon Madrid

Tagus River

Strait of *Gibraltar*

Africa

| 0 | 100 | 200 | 300 | 400 | 500 Miles |

© Rand McN
Made in U.S.A.
M-101049-4

What is
the symbol
for a country
capital?

R u s s i a

A s i a

60°

Sweden

Finland

rway

Oslo

Helsinki

Stockholm

Perm

Saint
Petersburg

Estonia

Moscow

Latvia

Lithuania

mark

nhagen

Russia

Minsk

K a z a k h s t a n

Berlin

Warsaw

Belarus

ermany

Poland

Kiev

Prague

Czechia

Ukraine

Volga River

Slovakia

Vienna

Budapest

Moldova

Austria

Hungary

Slovenia

Romania

Croatia

Belgrade

Bucharest

Bosnia and
Herzegovina

Danube River

Black Sea

Azerbaijan

Caspian Sea

Italy

Serbia

Montenegro

Kosovo

Bulgaria

Rome

Albania

North
Macedonia

Istanbul

T u r k e y

Greece

Athens

30°

Baltic Sea

Kama River

60°

30°

rranean
Sea

30°

Europe

———	Country boundary
∿	River
▨	Mountains
France	Country
⊛ Berlin	Country capital
■ Istanbul	City
Atlantic Ocean	Ocean

Asia

Asia is the largest continent.

Asia has more people than any other continent.

This is the Taj Mahal in India.

These are the Himalaya Mountains in Nepal.

This temple is in Thailand.

◀ This is a giant panda in China. Giant pandas spend most of the day eating!

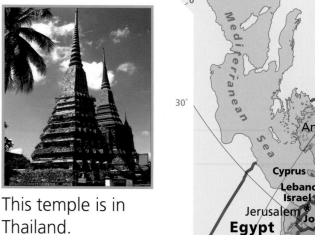

Mediterranean Sea

30°

Eu

Ankara ✱

Tur

Cyprus
Lebanon
Israel
Jerusalem ✱
Egypt

Africa

Jordan

Ku

Riyadh

Sau
Aral

30°

Yeme

Asia

———	Country boundary
‿	River
▨	Mountains
India	Country
✱ Bangkok	Country capital
■ Shanghai	City
Pacific Ocean	Ocean

Arctic Ocean

80°   60°

180°

pe
⊛ Moscow

R u s s i a

Ob River

Lena River

150°

30°

Kazakhstan

Ulaanbaatar ⊛

Japan

⊛ Tokyo

Uzbekistan

Mongolia

**North
Korea**

Turkmenistan

Beijing

⊛ Seoul

ad

Kyrgyzstan

**South
Korea**

⊛
Tehran

Tajikistan

C h i n a

Huang River

⊛ Shanghai

Pacific

in

Afghanistan

Kabul ⊛

Yangtze River

Ocean

Iran

⊛ Islamabad

Pakistan

Nepal

Ganges River

Bhutan

Taiwan

Oman

New
Karachi ■ Delhi

Guangzhou ■

■ Hong
Kong

Bangladesh

India   Kolkata ■

**Myanmar
(Burma) Laos**

Manila
⊛

Mumbai ■

Yangon

Thailand

Philippines

Arabian

Bay of

Vietnam

Sea   Bengaluru ■ ■ Chennai

Bengal Bangkok ⊛

Cambodia

■ Ho Chi
Minh City

Sri Lanka

Brunei

Malaysia

N

Indian

Kuala
Lumpur ⊛

■ Singapore

0°

Equator

W ⊛ E

I n d o n e s i a

Ocean

S

Jakarta

Timor-Leste

0   200 400 600 800 1000 Miles

⊛

Australia

© Rand McNally
Made in U.S.A.
M-101053-4

90°   120°

Africa

Africa is the warmest continent.

Map Skills

How many rivers can you find on the Africa map?

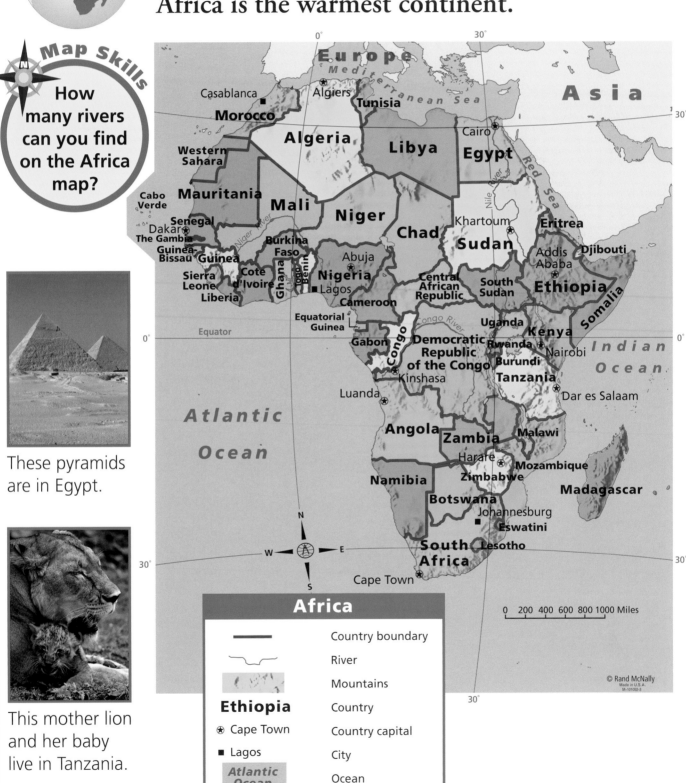

These pyramids are in Egypt.

This mother lion and her baby live in Tanzania.

Africa

——	Country boundary
⌇	River
▨	Mountains
Ethiopia	Country
⊛ Cape Town	Country capital
■ Lagos	City
Atlantic Ocean	Ocean

Map labels:
Europe, Asia, Mediterranean Sea, Casablanca, Algiers, Tunisia, Morocco, Algeria, Libya, Egypt, Cairo, Western Sahara, Cabo Verde, Mauritania, Mali, Niger, Chad, Sudan, Khartoum, Eritrea, Djibouti, Addis Ababa, Ethiopia, Somalia, Senegal, Dakar, The Gambia, Guinea-Bissau, Guinea, Burkina Faso, Abuja, Sierra Leone, Cote d'Ivoire, Ghana, Togo, Benin, Nigeria, Lagos, Cameroon, Central African Republic, South Sudan, Equatorial Guinea, Gabon, Congo, Democratic Republic of the Congo, Kinshasa, Congo River, Uganda, Rwanda, Burundi, Kenya, Nairobi, Tanzania, Dar es Salaam, Indian Ocean, Luanda, Angola, Zambia, Malawi, Harare, Zimbabwe, Mozambique, Madagascar, Namibia, Botswana, Johannesburg, Eswatini, South Africa, Lesotho, Cape Town, Atlantic Ocean, Equator, Nile River, Red Sea, Niger River

0 200 400 600 800 1000 Miles

© Rand McNally
Made in U.S.A.
M-101052-3

Australia

Australia is the smallest continent.
It is also a country.

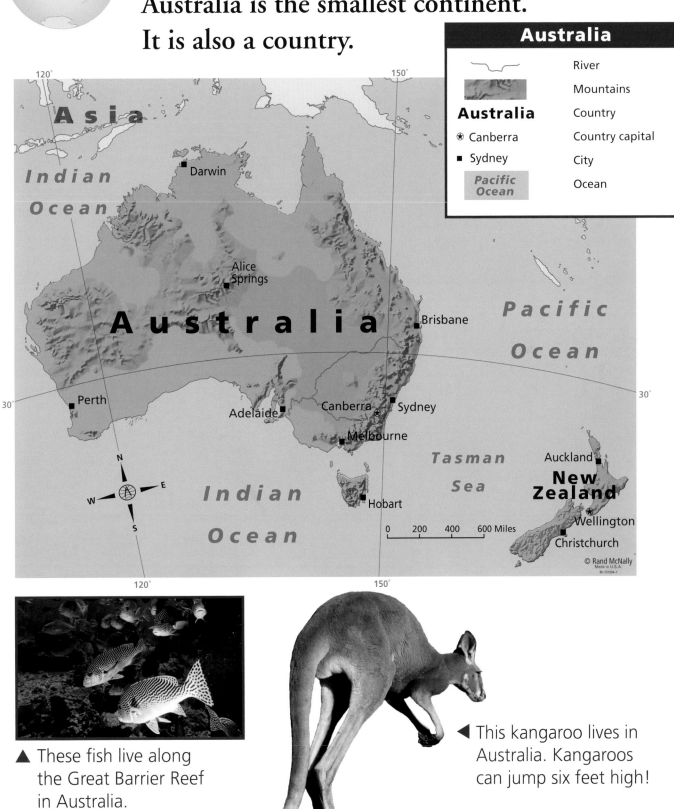

Australia

〜	River
▨	Mountains
Australia	Country
⊛ Canberra	Country capital
■ Sydney	City
Pacific Ocean	Ocean

A s i a

Indian Ocean

■ Darwin

A u s t r a l i a

Alice Springs

■ Brisbane

Pacific Ocean

■ Perth

Adelaide ■

Canberra ■ ⊛ ■ Sydney

■ Melbourne

Indian Ocean

■ Hobart

Tasman Sea

Auckland ■

New Zealand

⊛ Wellington

■ Christchurch

120° 150° 30°

N W E S

0   200   400   600 Miles

© Rand McNally
Made in U.S.A.
M-101054-1

▲ These fish live along the Great Barrier Reef in Australia.

◀ This kangaroo lives in Australia. Kangaroos can jump six feet high!

Antarctica

Antarctica is the coldest continent.

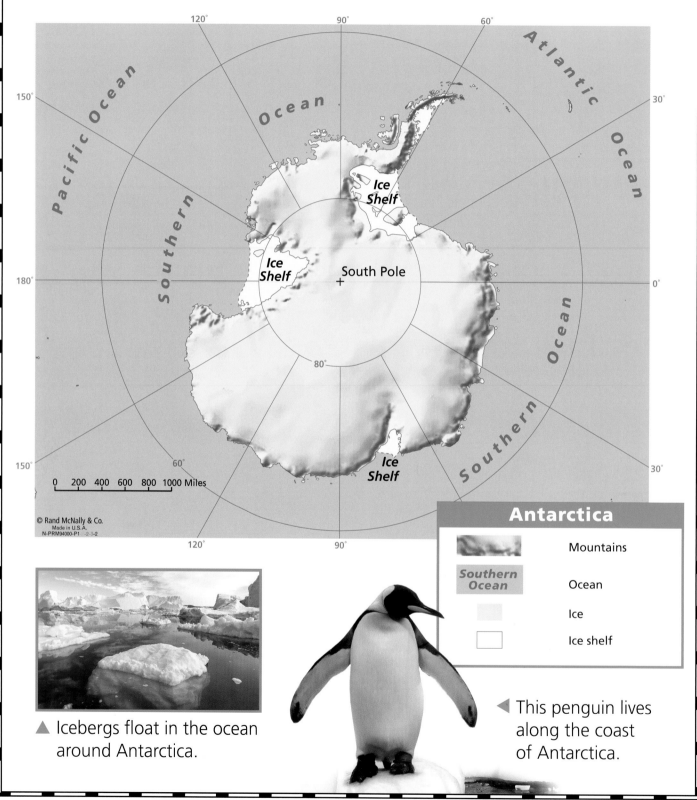

Atlantic Ocean

Pacific Ocean

Southern Ocean

Ocean

Southern Ocean

120°
90°
60°
150°
30°
180°
0°
150°
30°
120°
90°
80°

Ice Shelf

Ice Shelf

Ice Shelf

South Pole

0 200 400 600 800 1000 Miles

© Rand McNally & Co.
Made in U.S.A.
N-PRM94000-P1 -2-3-2

Antarctica

	Mountains
Southern Ocean	Ocean
	Ice
	Ice shelf

▲ Icebergs float in the ocean around Antarctica.

◀ This penguin lives along the coast of Antarctica.